PERFECT PICNICS

A Taste of Indulgence

PERFECT PICNICS

MARGARET O'SULLIVAN

CASSELL

First published in the UK in 1995 by
Cassell
Wellington House
125 Strand
London WC2R OBB

by arrangement with Lansdowne Publishing Pty Ltd
Level 5, 70 George Street, Sydney 2000, Australia

Managing Director: Jane Curry
Publishing Manager: Deborah Nixon
Production Manager: Sally Stokes
Project Co-ordinator: Pamela Brewster
Copy Editor: Lisa Foulis
Design: Modern Times Pty Ltd
Photographer: André Martin
Stylist: Donna Hay
Typeset in Garamond on Pagemaker
Printed in Singapore by Kyodo Printing Co. Pte

British Library Cataloguing-in-Publication Data
A catalogue record for this book is available from the British Library

ISBN 0-304-34757-4

Front cover: Miniature Frittatas, recipe page 57
Page 2: Zucchini (Courgette) Loaf, recipe page 109
Back cover: Scallop and Bell Pepper (Capsicum) Salad, recipe page 83

Contents

Introduction

FOOD DRIFTS up into another dimension when we eat outdoors: fresh air, the scent of grass and flowers, a feeling of freedom — all add their unique flavors. Our appetites are sharper too. In a natural setting the simplest food — good bread with ham and cheese, ripe peaches — becomes a banquet.

A picnic shouldn't resemble a home meal, although this was pretty much the case in England last century when the upper classes indulged their passion for picnics. Servants hurried ahead to set up tables — sometimes even tents — and they served food more suitable for a formal dining room.

But times have changed. Today, picnics are relaxed, happy affairs, and that means casual food that is simple to prepare, easy to transport and, above all, delicious and satisfying.

The word picnic comes from an 18th-century French word, *pique-nique* (from *piquer*: to pick, and *nique*: a small coin, or any little thing), which meant small pieces of food that could be picked up or picked at. Originally a picnic was an indoor or outdoor meal to which each guest brought a dish. In 19th-century London members of the exclusive Picnic Society got together to plan picnics and drew lots to decide what dish each member should contribute. This tradition survives today, with friends and families gathering outdoors and often sharing responsibility for the food.

Picnic food shouldn't be too subtle or elaborate; the sort of food you might serve at a special dinner party will only confuse the senses when you are revelling in the beauties of nature. And one of the joys of picnicking is escaping the drudgery of home chores — there's no point in making hard work of what should be a fun, carefree occasion.

This doesn't mean it's not worth making an effort to create a meal worthy of the setting — and appropriate too. If your picnic feast is destined for opera in the park, outdoor theatre or a crowded sporting fixture, choose something compact that doesn't require a lot of last-minute handling: for instance, chicken or smoked salmon sandwiches, fudge brownies, and a bottle of champagne. It may be worthwhile wrapping individual servings before you leave to save fuss and bother in a crowd. But if you are in the great outdoors with plenty of space you can really be creative.

A cold soup is a good start; it is easy to transport in a large jar or vacuum flask. There are many other starter options: miniature omelets, a platter of crudités with tapenade and aioli, vegetables stuffed with goat cheese, smoked salmon parcels with guacamole, or slices of that wonderful Mediterranean loaf, patafla — every one of them easy to pack and transport.

Barbecued meat or seafood makes a wonderful main course; there's nothing like the aroma of food cooking outdoors to stimulate the tastebuds. Steak, chops (cutlets), and sausages can go straight on the barbecue; lamb or pork kebabs and chicken will benefit from a marinade, which can be as simple as oil and dried herbs with perhaps some soy sauce, lemon juice, or wine. Seafood and some vegetables, such as eggplant (aubergine) and mushrooms, should be brushed with oil before barbecuing.

Potatoes take too long to cook if you start from scratch at a barbecue, but they keep warm for ages if you cook them before you leave home (by whatever method you prefer), and wrap them in foil and then in a towel. Give them another boost of heat — either in or out of their foil wrappings — when you get the barbecue going. Jacket roasted potatoes are great with a dollop of yogurt, sour cream, or butter mixed with chopped mint or parsley. Or try them with guacamole, tapenade, aioli, or store-bought chili and tomato salsa.

Ears of corn are also good outdoor fare. You can cook them at home in boiling water and finish them off on the barbecue after brushing them with oil or melted butter, or barbecue them in the husk after pulling out the silk.

A cold joint of meat is always excellent; you can carve it at home and wrap it in foil to transport. Substantial Asian-style salads (see Thai Beef Salad, page 91, and Chinese Duck Salad, page 31) make a nice change from traditional picnic food, and they have the added advantage of being self-contained. Egg dishes are good too — frittatas are perfect for picnics — as are old favorites such as egg and bacon pie.

And don't forget the not-so-humble sandwich. A wide range of wonderful breads, including pita and focaccia, have lifted the sandwich into the gourmet class.

Let everyone assemble their own. Take two or three different types of bread and a selection of individually packed fillings. Choose from hot and mild salami, ham, prosciutto, pastrami, corned beef, rare roast beef, cold roast lamb or pork, paté, terrines, meatballs, cheese (including marinated feta or baby bocconcinis), sun-dried tomatoes, marinated mushrooms and eggplant (aubergine), guacamole, falafel, hommos, tabbouleh, taramasalata, chicken, home-made mayonnaise, hard-cooked (hard-boiled) eggs mashed with anchovies and mayonnaise, olives, smoked salmon, salad greens, thinly sliced onions, cucumbers and bell peppers (capsicums), tomatoes, pickles, mustards, and relishes.

Or whatever! Obviously you can't bring the lot, but try to offer contrast and compatibility — for instance, brown bread with smoked salmon, cream cheese, onion rings, and capers, or pita with meatballs, hommos, tabbouleh and salad greens. Consider also the possibilities of chopped nuts mixed with dried fruit and cheese; for example, chopped pecans, dates, and cheddar, or cream cheese, dried figs, and walnuts.

Many sandwiches can be made in advance and even frozen if made a day or more ahead. Chicken with herb mayonnaise, smoked salmon with caper butter, and paté sandwiches are particularly suitable for freezing.

Elaborate desserts are out of place outdoors, but it's essential to have some sort of sweet treat. Home-made cookies, fudge brownies, a cake that carries well, or delicious fresh fruit are ideal. Or choose a cake that can be frozen in advance — something from the supermarket freezer that will help keep other food cold as you travel to your chosen picnic destination.

Don't take your best china and glassware, but it's handy to have a couple of serving platters and essential to pack a salad bowl (carry salad dressing in a small glass jar and salad greens in plastic bags in a cold box). Keep everything that needs to be kept cold chilled with freezer icepacks. Then sit back and enjoy the warmth of being alive ...

THE RECIPES

Anchovy Eggs

6 hard-cooked (hard-boiled) eggs,
   shelled
6 anchovy fillets, roughly chopped,
   in their oil
1 tablespoon mayonnaise

1 teaspoon tomato paste (passata)
1 tablespoon finely chopped dill
   pickle (gherkin)
black pepper

ANCHOVY EGGS are a wonderful addition to an antipasto platter of olives, paté, baby bocconcinis, marinated mushrooms, sun-dried tomatoes or tomatoes with basil and virgin olive oil, and salami.

Slice the eggs in half and scoop out the yolks into a bowl. Add the anchovy fillets, mayonnaise, tomato paste, and dill pickle to the bowl and mash together. Divide the mixture between the eggs to fill.

Keep cold in an air-tight container until ready to serve.

Serves 6

M • E • N • U

•

Anchovy Eggs

•

*Smoked Salmon
with Capers and
Vinegar Onions*

•

*Zucchini (Courgette) Loaf
(page 109)*

•

*Fudge Brownies
(page 43)*

•

Apple Cake

2 eggs
½ cup (4 oz/125 g) sugar
¼ cup (2 fl oz/60 ml) milk
3 teaspoons vanilla extract (essence)
2 oz (60 g) butter, melted
1 cup (5 oz/150 g) self-rising
   (raising) flour, sifted

6 teaspoons cornstarch (cornflour),
   sifted
1 large green apple, peeled, cored,
   and sliced
1½ teaspoons cinnamon mixed
   with extra sugar for topping

GREASE and line an 8 inch (20 cm) cake pan with non-stick parchment (baking paper).

Beat the eggs and sugar until thick and pale. Stir in the milk, vanilla extract, and butter. Add the flour and cornstarch and beat lightly. Pour the mixture into the prepared pan. Decoratively arrange apple slices on the top and sprinkle with cinnamon sugar.

Bake in a moderately hot oven (375°F/190°C/Gas Mark 5) for about 35 minutes or until a wooden skewer inserted in the middle comes out clean.

This cake can be served warm; otherwise, cool on a cake rack.

Serves 6

Asparagus and Dill Soup

1 leek
6 tablespoons oil
½ teaspoon salt
15 asparagus stalks

4 cups (32 fl oz /1 L) chicken stock
fresh dill, chopped
yogurt or thick cream, optional

M • E • N • U
•
Asparagus and Dill Soup
•
Stuffed Duck in Aspic
(page 89)
•
Minted Orange Salad
(page 61)
•
Honey Wafers
(page 51)
•

THIS soup is equally delicious served hot or cold.

Cut off most, but not all, of the green part of the leek, then make two cross-cuts almost to the root. Rinse well in a sink full of water. Chop finely.

Heat the oil in a heavy saucepan and add the leek and salt. Stir, then cover and cook gently until the leek softens, stirring occasionally.

Break the tough end off each asparagus stalk and discard, then finely slice the stalks except for the tips. Set the tips aside. Add the sliced stalks to the leek, stir and continue cooking for about 5 minutes until the asparagus starts to soften.

Transfer to a food processor or blender, add a little of the chicken stock and purée.

Return the purée to the saucepan with the rest of the chicken stock and the asparagus tips, and bring gently to a simmer, stirring occasionally.

Add a generous amount of fresh dill and serve hot or chilled. A dollop of good quality yogurt or cream can also be added if desired.

Serves 4

Avocados with Rum and Lime Juice

3 teaspoons rum
juice of 2 limes
1 pinch salt

black pepper
2 avocados

PUT the rum, lime juice, salt, and black pepper in a jar and shake to mix.

Just before you are ready to eat, cut the avocados in half, remove the seeds and fill the halves with the dressing.

Serves 4

Strawberries with Balsamic Vinegar

about 1 punnet (8 oz /250 g)
    strawberries

1 tablespoon balsamic vinegar, or to
    taste

THIS is ultra-simple picnic fare, requiring hardly any advance preparation. About 30 minutes before serving, slice the strawberries in half and sprinkle with balsamic vinegar (you can adjust the amount to taste).

Serve this dish with Avocados with Rum and Lime Juice.

Serves 2–3

Baked Ricotta

4 tablespoons olive oil
1 small green bell pepper (capsicum),
   finely sliced in rings
1 fresh ricotta cheese
   (about 8 oz/250 g)

6 sun-dried tomatoes, marinated in
   oil, roughly chopped
1 teaspoon dried oregano
black pepper

HEAT 1 tablespoon of the olive oil in a pan and sauté the bell pepper for about 5 minutes until soft.

Slice the fresh ricotta cheese in half horizontally and place the bottom half on an oiled baking sheet.

Spread the bell pepper and sun-dried tomatoes evenly over the bottom half of the ricotta. Sprinkle with some of the marinade oil from the sun-dried tomatoes, then with the oregano and black pepper to taste. Top with the other half of the ricotta. Spoon the remaining 3 tablespoons olive oil over the top, and sprinkle again with black pepper.

Cover with foil and bake in a moderately hot oven (375°F/190°C/Gas Mark 5) for 15 minutes. Take out of the oven and remove the foil. Using your hands, press down gently on the ricotta to ensure the two halves stay together and keep a compact shape. Continue cooking, without foil, for another 15–20 minutes until a pale gold.

Serve warm or at room temperature. This dish will keep well in the refrigerator for up to 1 week.

Serves 4–6

Barbecued Atlantic Salmon with Pesto Dressing

PESTO

1 bunch basil

4 oz (125 g) walnuts

2 cloves garlic

¼ cup (2 fl oz/60 ml) olive oil

2 fl oz (60 ml) light (single) cream

2 fillets Atlantic salmon
   (about 6 oz/180 g each)

2 tablespoons olive oil

1 bell pepper (capsicum), finely sliced

PESTO is more versatile if you make it without the usual addition of Parmesan cheese. If a Parmesan taste is desired, for instance with pasta, the Parmesan can be added separately. This quantity is more than you need, but it freezes well.

To make the pesto put the leaves and some of the tender stalks of the basil into a food processor or blender. Add the remaining ingredients and process. Store the pesto in a jar and keep in the refrigerator or freezer. Make a dressing by mixing half the pesto with the cream.

Brush the salmon fillets with the olive oil and cook the pink side for 2 minutes on a barbecue, then turn to cook the skin side for about 3 minutes.

Serve the salmon fillets with the pesto and cream dressing and a few slices of bell pepper on the side.

NOTE: Salmon is also good served cold with Pesto Dressing, so if necessary you can cook it at home before leaving.

Serves 2

Barbecued Double Lamb Cutlets with Ratatouille

8 double lamb cutlets (ask the
    butcher to cut these, or cut them
    yourself from racks of lamb)
dried oregano
¼ cup (4 fl oz/125 ml) soy sauce
salad greens and fresh mint, to serve
RATATOUILLE
8 tablespoons olive oil

2 onions, chopped
1 large eggplant (aubergine), diced
1 bell pepper (capsicum), diced
½ teaspoon salt
4 tomatoes, chopped
6 cloves garlic, finely chopped
1 teaspoon ground coriander

M • E • N • U
•
Avocados with Rum and
Lime Juice
(page 17)
•
Barbecued Double Lamb
Cutlets with Ratatouille
•
Cheese and Crackers
•

JUST before you leave home, sprinkle the lamb cutlets with dried oregano and soy sauce and marinate for no longer than an hour or so.

Cook on a barbecue for about 6 minutes per side. If it's not convenient to barbecue you can cook the meat at home in a corrugated cast-iron pan and wrap it in foil, but in this case the meat needs to be very well trimmed of fat.

To make the Ratatouille heat the olive oil in a heavy saucepan, add the onions and cook until they start to soften. Add the eggplant, bell pepper, and salt. Cover the saucepan and continue cooking, stirring regularly with a wooden spoon, until the vegetables soften. Add the tomatoes, garlic, and ground coriander and continue cooking, covered, for about 30 minutes until the vegetables have melted together, stirring regularly to prevent sticking. If the mixture seems too liquid continue cooking uncovered for another 5 minutes.

Serve the cutlets with salad greens, including some fresh mint, and cold Ratatouille on the side.

Serves 4

Barbecued Quail

MARINADE
½ cup (4 fl oz/125 ml) vegetable
  oil
2 tablespoons sweet chili sauce
2 tablespoons balsamic vinegar
1 tablespoon Thai fish sauce
1 tablespoon packed (soft) brown sugar
4 garlic cloves, finely chopped

2 teaspoons finely chopped fresh
  ginger
8 quail, halved
SALAD
6 cups (8 oz/250 g) mixed salad greens
4 sun-dried tomatoes, chopped
fresh chervil or cilantro (fresh
  coriander), if unobtainable

M • E • N • U
•
Vegetables Stuffed with
Goat Cheese
(page 97)
•
Barbecued Quail
•
Cold Fruit Pie
•

NOTHING beats the taste and aroma of food cooked in the open air; however, if it's not possible to barbecue, don't let that deter you. The quail can be broiled (grilled) at home, the marinade heated and transferred to a jar, then put together with the salad when you get to the picnic destination.

Mix the marinade ingredients together, put the quail into a non-reactive bowl, and pour the marinade over. Cover and leave overnight.

Barbecue or broil (grill) the quail for about 5 minutes each side, reserving the marinade.

Put the marinade into a saucepan and bring to a boil. Cool slightly, then pour into a jar ready to take to the picnic or if you are preparing this at the picnic then immediately toss the marinade through the mixed salad greens and the sun-dried tomatoes.

Divide the salad between four plates, add the quail and garnish with fresh chervil.

Serves 4

Blueberry Sour Cream Cake

4 oz (125 g) butter, softened
1 cup (8 oz/250 g) superfine (caster)
  sugar
2 eggs, lightly beaten
1 teaspoon vanilla extract (essence)

2 cups (10 oz/300 g) self-rising
  (raising) flour, sifted
⅔ cup (6 fl oz/180 ml) sour cream
10 oz (300 g) fresh or frozen
  blueberries

CREAM the butter and sugar until light and fluffy. Beat in the egg and the
vanilla extract. Fold in the flour and the sour cream. Gently stir half the
blueberries into the cake mixture and scrape it into a greased 9 inch (23 cm)
springform cake pan. Sprinkle the remaining blueberries evenly over the top
of the mixture.

Bake in a moderate oven (350°F/180°C/Gas Mark 4) for 50 minutes
until the top is firm and slightly browned or until a wooden skewer inserted
in the middle comes out clean.

Cool in the cake pan.

Serves 8

Chili Plum Sauce

2 lb (1 kg) plums, roughly chopped
1 onion, chopped
2 oz (60 g) golden raisins (sultanas)
1 teaspoon each allspice, peppercorns and mustard seeds (black or white)
½ teaspoon cayenne pepper
1 inch (2.5 cm) piece of fresh ginger root, crushed

6 small red chilies, seeded and chopped
1¼ cups (10 fl oz/300 ml) malt vinegar
1 teaspoon salt
4 oz (125 g) packed (soft) brown sugar

THIS sauce is great with Oriental Meatballs (see page 67), or barbecued pork or beef spare ribs.

Put the plums and onion into a saucepan with the raisins, spices, ginger, chilies and half the vinegar. Bring to a boil, then simmer gently for 30 minutes, or until the plums are soft and pulpy.

Rub the mixture through a sieve or colander, then return the sauce to the pan, discarding the seeds etc that do not go through the sieve.

Add the remaining vinegar, salt and sugar. Bring to a boil, stirring, until the sugar has dissolved.

Simmer uncovered, stirring occasionally, for about 1 hour or until the sauce starts to thicken.

Pour into bottles or jars (see note, page 73) and seal at once.

Makes about 3 lb (1½ kg)

Chinese Duck Salad

1 cucumber, finely sliced
salt
2 teaspoons sugar
1 tablespoon white wine vinegar
4 oz (125 g) snow peas (mangetout)
4 oz (125 g) bean sprouts
1 purple (Spanish) onion, finely sliced
½ red bell pepper (capsicum), cut
   into julienne

1 zucchini (courgette), cut into
   julienne
6 button mushrooms, finely sliced
2 tablespoons walnut oil
juice of half a lemon
1 Chinese barbecued duck, chopped
   into serving pieces

FOR this recipe you need to have access to the barbecued ducks sold in some Chinese supermarkets. Ask the storekeeper to chop it for you.

Spread the cucumber on paper towels, then sprinkle with salt and cover with more paper towels. Press down to extract some of the liquid and leave for 10 minutes. Transfer the cucumber to a colander and rinse under cold water. Put the cucumber into a jar, add the sugar and vinegar, cover and shake.

Cook the snow peas in boiling water for 5 minutes, drain and spread out on a board to dry. Put the snow peas into a container with the remaining ingredients except the cucumber and duck, mix together and cover.

At the picnic drain the cucumber and mix it in with the other vegetables. You can either toss the duck into the salad vegetables or serve it on a bed of salad.

NOTE: Cucumber prepared as above makes a lovely salad on its own.

Serves 4

Cold Avocado Soup

2 avocados, halved and seeds removed
1 small white onion, chopped
2 cups (16 fl oz/500 ml) chicken
  stock

1 cup (8 fl oz/250 ml) buttermilk
salt and freshly ground black pepper
1 red bell pepper (capsicum), halved
1 teaspoon Tabasco sauce

A RICH, cold soup is a lovely start to a summer picnic; it is easy to carry in a large glass jar or vacuum flask.

Scrape the avocado flesh into a food processor or blender. Add the onion and stock and process until smooth.

Pour into a container and stir in the buttermilk and salt and pepper to taste. Put aside until ready to serve.

Put the bell pepper under a broiler (griller) until the skin blackens. Transfer to a paper bag and leave for about 30 minutes. Scrape off the blackened skin. Put the bell pepper into a food processor or blender with the Tabasco and purée. Transfer to a small jar.

To serve, add a dollop of the bell pepper purée to each bowl of avocado soup.

Serves 4

M • E • N • U
•
Cold Avocado Soup
•
*Scallop and Bell Pepper
(Capsicum) Salad
(page 83)*
•
Cookies
•

Cold Omelets

6 large eggs   *filling (see below)*
olive oil

MAKE 6 individual omelets: Beat 1 egg lightly. Heat a small amount of olive oil in a small non-stick pan over medium heat, then add the egg to the pan. As it starts to set, add about 1 tablespoon of filling to one side. Fold over and remove from the pan.

Serves 6

FILLING SUGGESTIONS
Chopped smoked salmon, Ratatouille (see page 23), sautéed sliced mushrooms, cream cheese and herbs, sautéed sliced bell pepper (capsicum), chopped tomato that has been skinned and seeded, salmon roe, sautéed asparagus tips.

M • E • N • U
•
Duck Liver Paté and French Bread
(page 37)
•
Cold Omelets
•
Waldorf Salad
(page 61)
•
Apple Cake
(page 13)
•

Duck Liver Paté

1 oz (30 g) butter
1 onion, chopped
1 clove garlic, chopped
8 oz (250 g) trimmed duck livers

2–3 sprigs fresh sage, chopped
3 teaspoons brandy
salt and black pepper
3 oz (90 g) butter, extra, melted

FRESH sage turns this easy-to-make paté into gourmet fare. If unobtainable, substitute another fresh herb, such as thyme, oregano, or marjoram, or 1 teaspoon dried sage.

Melt butter in a pan and sauté the onion and garlic over low heat for about 5 minutes until the onion starts to soften.

Add the duck livers and cook for 4–5 minutes, stirring occasionally, until brown on the outside but still pink inside. Add the sage, stir through the duck livers, then set aside to cool.

Transfer to a food processor or blender, add the brandy, salt and black pepper, and about two-thirds of the extra melted butter; process until smooth.

Transfer the paté to a dish, smooth the surface and top with the remaining melted butter.

Serves 4–6

Egg and Bacon Pie

1 sheet ready-rolled pie crust
  (shortcrust) pastry
1 tablespoon olive oil
6 bacon strips (rashers), rind
  removed
1 green bell pepper (capsicum), cut
  into thin strips

4 teaspoons tomato paste (passata)
6 eggs
2 oz (60 g) feta cheese
2 oz (60 g) ricotta cheese
½ teaspoon nutmeg
¼ cup (2 fl oz/60 ml) light (single) cream
black pepper

HERE is a new version of this traditional picnic dish, incorporating feta and ricotta cheese. A mixed green salad is the only accompaniment you need.

Line a greased pie dish with the pastry; use a fork to prick some holes in the bottom and bake in a moderate oven (350°F/180°C/ Gas Mark 4) for 15 minutes, or until lightly browned. Set aside to cool.

Meanwhile, heat the olive oil in a frying pan, and fry the bacon. Remove and set aside to cool. In the same pan, gently sauté the bell pepper for about 5 minutes, until it starts to soften. Set aside to cool.

Spread the tomato paste over the bottom of the pastry shell. Break 3 of the eggs (either whole or with yolks broken) into the pastry shell, then add some of the bell pepper, bacon, and cheeses. Sprinkle with nutmeg.

Add the remaining eggs then the remaining bell pepper, bacon, and cheeses, so that you have a roughly even mix.

Pour the cream over the top, then grind on some black pepper. Bake in a moderately hot oven (375°F/190°C/Gas Mark 5) for about 30 minutes until the mixture is set and golden.

Serves 6

Egg and Caviar Paté

8 hard-cooked (hard-boiled) eggs
2 oz (60 g) butter, cut into small
    pieces
1½ cups (10 fl oz/300 ml) sour
    cream

1 small white onion, finely chopped
5 oz (150 g) red lumpfish roe
5 oz (150 g) black lumpfish roe

PROCESS the eggs, butter, sour cream, and white onion in a food processor or blender just long enough to blend.

Spread the mixture into a paté dish and chill in the refrigerator until firm.

Cover half the surface with red lumpfish roe and the other half with black lumpfish roe. (You can, of course, use all red or all black lumpfish roe, or more of one than the other.)

Cover with plastic (cling) wrap and keep cold until serving time; serve with bread or crackers.

Serves 8

M • E • N • U
•
Egg and Caviar Paté
•
*Glazed Pickled Pork
with Cumberland Sauce
(page 45)*
•
*Watermelon
and Lychee Salad
(page 103)*
•

Fudge Brownies

4 oz (125 g) semi-sweet (plain)
    chocolate, chopped
8 oz (250 g) butter
2 cups (1 lb/500 g) sugar
3 eggs

2 teaspoons rum
1 cup (5 oz/150 g) all-purpose
    (plain) flour, sifted
½ teaspoon salt
1 cup (4 oz/125 g) chopped pecans

PUT the chocolate and half the butter in a bowl over hot water and stir until melted. Set aside to cool.

Cream the remaining butter with the sugar until light and fluffy. Add the eggs, one at a time, and beat. Add the rum and stir, then add the chocolate and stir into the mixture.

Add the flour, salt, and pecans and stir to combine.

Pour into a greased shallow cake pan (about 12 x 10 inch/30 x 25 cm) and bake in a moderate oven (350°F/180°C/Gas Mark 4) for 45 minutes, or until a skewer inserted in the middle comes out clean.

Cool in the pan. Cut into squares to serve.

M • E • N • U
•
Cold Avocado Soup
(page 33)
•
Barbecued Quail
(page 25)
•
Fudge Brownies
•

Glazed Pickled Pork

10 lb (5 kg) piece of pickled (pumped)
    pork butt (pork leg)
2 tablespoons packed (soft) brown
    sugar
2 tablespoons vinegar
1 carrot, chopped
1 onion, quartered
peel (rind) of 1 lemon
1 teaspoon black peppercorns
1 orange, studded with cloves

parsley
extra cloves
GLAZE
1 cup (8 oz/250 g) sugar
½ cup (4 fl oz/125 ml) honey
2 tablespoons dry mustard
1 tablespoon sherry
GARNISH
chopped fresh herbs
thin strips of orange peel (rind)

CUMBERLAND SAUCE
•
6 tablespoons
redcurrant jelly

2 tablespoons lemon juice

2 tablespoons orange
marmalade

4 tablespoons port wine

2 teaspoons prepared
English mustard

Combine all of the
ingredients. Serve cold.
•

THIS is magnificently eye-catching for an outdoor feast.

Put the pork in a large pot with the remaining ingredients, except the
extra cloves, and cover with cold water. Bring slowly to a boil (this takes
about 1 hour), then simmer for 2 hours 20 minutes. (Allow a total cooking
time after it comes to a boil of about 20 minutes per 1 lb/500 g — including
the hour in the oven at the end.)

Remove the pork from the pot. Set aside until it is cool enough to pull off
the skin, leaving a layer of fat. Use a sharp knife to score the fat in a diamond
pattern. Stud with the extra cloves. Mix the glaze ingredients together to
form a stiff paste. Cover the pork well with the glaze. Bake in a moderately
hot oven (400°F/200°C/Gas Mark 6) for 1 hour, basting occasionally.

Remove from the oven and serve with Cumberland Sauce. Decorate with
some chopped fresh herbs and thin strips of orange peel if desired.

Serves 12–15

Greek Salad Skewers

8 large cherry tomatoes   *fresh oregano*
16 large black olives, pitted   *virgin olive oil*
8 oz (250 g) Greek feta cheese, cubed

SALAD on a stick is a useful idea for picnics. Try to find the real Greek feta cheese, but don't be deterred if you have to use a local feta.

Divide the cherry tomatoes, black olives, and feta cheese between 8 small wooden skewers.

Transfer to a container and sprinkle with oregano and olive oil.

Serves 4

M • E • N • U
•
Tapenade with Crudités
(page 95)
•
Walnut Chicken
(page 101)
•
Wild Rice Salad
(page 105)
•
Greek Salad Skewers
•
Apple Cake
(page 13)
•

Herbed Eye Fillet

1 oz (30 g) butter
crushed black peppercorns
1 eye fillet of beef, about 2 lb (1 kg)
¼ cup (2 fl oz/60 ml) brandy,
    optional

2 tablespoons capers, chopped
2 cloves garlic, finely chopped
fresh parsley, finely chopped

MELT the butter in a baking dish on top of the stove. Press some peppercorns into the beef.

Turn up the heat under the baking dish and quickly sear the beef on all sides. If using brandy, add it to the pan and flame it as the fumes start to rise. Remove from the heat. Combine the capers, garlic, and parsley and press into the surface of the seared beef.

Roast in a moderately hot oven (400°F/200°C/Gas Mark 6) for about 30 minutes or until cooked as desired (30 minutes per 2 lb/1 kg for rare, 40 minutes per 2 lb/1 kg for medium).

Leave the meat to rest for 15 minutes before carving.

Serves 6

Honey Wafers

4 oz (125 g) butter, softened
6 oz (180 g) superfine (caster) sugar
2 tablespoons honey

3 oz (90 g) all-purpose (plain) flour, sifted
2 egg whites

THESE wafers are a delight on their own, or they can be sandwiched together with any cake frosting or filling. They are also good with icecream.

Cream the butter and sugar until light and fluffy. Stir in the honey and flour.

In a separate bowl, beat the egg whites until white and frothy. Stir the egg whites into the mixture.

Line two baking sheets with parchment (baking paper) and drop spoonfuls of the mixture onto the trays — leave room in between for the wafers to spread to about 3 inches (7½ cm) across. You will probably have to cook the mixture in two batches.

Bake in a moderate oven (350°F/180°C/Gas Mark 4) for about 15 minutes until golden brown.

Leave to cool for about 1 minute on the baking sheets then transfer to a cake rack to finish cooling.

Keep in an air-tight container.

Makes about 16

Ida's Aberdeen Sausage

1 lb (500 g) ground (minced) beef
   steak (top quality with little fat)
8 oz (250 g) bacon, ground (minced)
1 egg, beaten

1 tablespoon tomato paste (passata)
2 cups (6 oz/180 g) fresh breadcrumbs
salt and black pepper
fresh breadcrumbs, extra, for serving

THIS recipe was my mother-in-law's specialty for family picnics. It's delicious served with Potato Salad (page 75) and some crusty bread.

Combine the ground steak, bacon, egg, tomato paste, breadcrumbs, and salt and black pepper to taste.

Shape the mixture into a roll on a lightly floured work surface. Wrap the roll securely in foil.

Put into a pot of boiling water, cover, and leave to simmer for 2 hours.

To serve, cool, then roll in extra breadcrumbs and cut into thin slices.

Serves 6

M • E • N • U
•
Anchovy Eggs
(page 11)
•
Ida's Aberdeen Sausage
•
Potato Salad
(page 75)
•
Blueberry Sour Cream
Cake
(page 27)
•

Kumera, Banana, and Avocado Salad

2 medium kumeras (sweet potato)
peeled and cut into bite-sized
cubes
1 large banana, sliced
1 avocado, diced

½ cup (4 fl oz/125 ml) mayonnaise
¼ cup (2 fl oz/60 ml) plain yogurt
1–2 teaspoons curry powder, to taste
2 oz (60 g) pecan nuts, chopped

THIS tropical salad is excellent with cold chicken or cold roast pork. If desired, you can add some pineapple cubes.

Boil or steam the kumera until tender, but still firm. Set aside to cool.

Put the banana and avocado into a bowl. Combine the mayonnaise, yogurt, and curry powder, then add to the banana and avocado. Add the cooled kumera and stir lightly to mix.

Just before serving, sprinkle chopped pecan nuts over the top.

Serves 4–6

Miniature Frittatas

4 oz (125 g) smoked salmon, finely
  chopped
3 oz (90 g) goat cheese, crumbled
fresh chives, chopped

6 eggs
¼ cup (2 fl oz/60 ml) single (light)
  cream

THESE miniature frittatas make a great picnic starter — serve them with chilled champagne. You can vary the fillings: chopped artichoke hearts, prosciutto, asparagus tips, Ratatouille (page 23), sautéed mushrooms or leek, or smoked salmon and goat cheese as combined here.

Grease a 12 cup cake (patty cake) pan. Divide the smoked salmon, goat cheese, and chives between the cups.

Lightly beat the eggs with the cream and pour into the cups.

Bake in a moderately hot oven (400°F/200°C/Gas Mark 6) for 8–10 minutes until golden brown.

Turn onto a cake cooler and serve at room temperature.

Serves 4–6

M • E • N • U
•
Miniature Frittatas
•
*Barbecued Double Lamb
Cutlets with Ratatouille
(page 23)*
•
*Honey Wafers
(page 51)*
•

Minted Eggplant (Aubergine)

1 eggplant (aubergine)
olive oil
½ cup (4 fl oz/125 ml) white wine
   vinegar

3 cloves garlic, chopped
leaves from 4 sprigs mint, chopped

THIS dish goes well with barbecued lamb or cold roast lamb; it is also very good in pita sandwiches with slices of roast lamb.

Cut the eggplant into slices a bit less than ½ inch (1 cm) thick. Spread the eggplant over a clean cloth on a tray and take out into the sun to dry for about 1 hour.

Alternatively, you can dry the eggplant in a microwave: spread some paper towels on the microwave turntable and cover with the eggplant. Microwave for about 5 minutes on low, then turn the slices over and microwave for another 5 minutes on low. At the end of the process the eggplant should be soft rather than firm to touch.

Heat enough oil to cover the bottom of a frying pan and fry the eggplant over a medium heat on each side; do this in stages, adding more oil as necessary. Drain on paper towels to soak up the excess oil.

Put the vinegar into a bowl, add the eggplant and toss through. Leave in the vinegar for about 2 minutes, then lift out the eggplant slices and transfer to a platter. Sprinkle with the garlic and mint and cover with plastic (cling) wrap until ready to serve.

Serves 6

Minted Orange Salad and Waldorf Salad

MINTED ORANGE SALAD
6 oranges
1 tablespoon white wine vinegar
3 tablespoons olive oil
¼ teaspoon salt
fresh mint

WALDORF SALAD
1 tablespoon mayonnaise
1 tablespoon plain yogurt
2 apples, cored and diced
1 stick celery, sliced
1 oz (30 g) pecans
1 oz (30 g) grapes

THERE is nothing ordinary about apples and oranges in the following refreshing salads.

MINTED ORANGE SALAD
Squeeze the juice from 1 orange and pour into a bowl. Mix in vinegar, olive oil, and salt. Peel the remaining oranges so that none of the pith remains and cut into thick slices. Add to the bowl and toss lightly. Remove sprigs from the top of each mint stalk, then strip the leaves off the rest of the stalk. Add mint sprigs and leaves to the salad just before serving and toss together.

WALDORF SALAD
MIX together the mayonnaise and yogurt. Put all of the remaining ingredients in a bowl and mix together. Add the mayonnaise mixture and toss. Serve chilled.

This salad is excellent with cold roast chicken.

Serves 4–6

Mushroom Salad

½ cup (4 fl oz/125 ml) virgin
   olive oil
6 anchovy fillets, drained
2 tablespoons lemon juice
1 bunch parsley, coarse stems
   removed

2 cloves garlic
black pepper
12 oz (375 g) mushrooms,
   finely sliced

THIS salad is delicious with barbecued steaks, potatoes in their jackets, and
a mixed green salad.

Put all the ingredients except the mushrooms into a food processor or
blender and process until the parsley is finely chopped and combined with
the other ingredients. Or alternatively finely chop the anchovies, parsley
and garlic and combine with the oil, lemon juice and black pepper.

Put the mushrooms into a bowl and add the dressing. Mix well and
leave for at least 30 minutes before serving.

Serves 4–6

Oriental Cucumber Salad

1 long cucumber
1 teaspoon finely chopped fresh
   ginger
1 tablespoon white wine vinegar
1 tablespoon vegetable oil
1 teaspoon sesame oil

1 tablespoon soy sauce
1 teaspoon wasabi
1 teaspoon packed (soft) brown
   sugar
2 oz (60 g) bean sprouts
cilantro (fresh coriander) leaves

PEEL the cucumber, cut down the middle and scrape out the seeds, then cut into slices slightly under ½ inch (1 cm) wide.

Mix the remaining ingredients, except the bean sprouts and cilantro, in a bowl, add the cucumber slices and leave for about 2 hours.

Just before serving, toss in the bean sprouts and cilantro.

Serves 4

M • E • N • U
•
Asparagus and Dill Soup
(page 15)
•
Barbecued Quail
(page 25)
•
Oriental Cucumber Salad
•
Fruit and Cheese
•

Oriental Meatballs

1 oz (30 g) dried mushrooms
2 lb (1 kg) ground (minced) pork or
    beef
3 oz (90 g) water chestnuts, finely
    chopped
4 oz (125 g) bacon, finely chopped
2 cloves garlic, finely chopped

3 teaspoons finely chopped fresh
    ginger
1 onion, finely chopped
3 teaspoons chili sauce
¼ cup (2 fl oz/60 ml) soy sauce
3 tablespoons vegetable oil

M • E • N • U
•
Oriental Meatballs with
Chili Plum Sauce
(page 29)
•
Egg and Bacon Pie
(page 39)
•
Mixed Green Salad
•
Fruit
•

COLD meatballs make wonderful picnic fare served with Chili Plum Sauce (see page 29). This adaptable mixture can also be shaped into hamburger patties and barbecued, or baked as meatloaf (about 45 minutes at 350°F/ 180°C/Gas Mark 4) and served hot or cold.

Soak the mushrooms in warm water for about 30 minutes. Drain and chop finely.

Use your hands to thoroughly combine the remaining ingredients except the vegetable oil in a bowl. Shape into balls.

Heat the vegetable oil in a frying pan and fry the meatballs, turning to brown on each side. Do this in stages so that the pan is not too crowded. Drain each batch on paper towels. If necessary add more oil.

Serve hot or cold.

Serves 8

Pan Bagnia

6 tablespoons olive oil
4 large slices eggplant (aubergine)
16 French beans
4 bread rolls
8 teaspoons olive oil, extra
2 cloves garlic, finely chopped
parsley, finely chopped

1 red bell pepper (capsicum), cut
  into strips
12 black olives, pitted
16 slices prosciutto
1 purple (Spanish) onion, thinly
  sliced, optional

M • E • N • U
•
Tomato and Buttermilk
Soup
(page 93)
•
Pan Bagnia
•
Fudge Brownies
(page 43)
•

HEAT 6 tablespoons of olive oil in a frying pan and fry the eggplant slices until golden brown on each side. Lift out and drain on paper towels.

Cook the beans in boiling water for 5 minutes. Drain.

Cut the bread rolls in half and brush the cut surfaces with extra olive oil.

Sprinkle the bottom half of each bread roll with the garlic and parsley, then add a slice of eggplant to each one. Divide the remaining ingredients, including the beans, between the bread rolls, then join the halves of the bread rolls together.

Wrap each bread roll securely in plastic (cling) wrap, then put all four under a heavy weight (such as a heavy bread board) for about 30 minutes.

Serves 4

Patafla

4 tomatoes

1 large purple (Spanish) onion,
    finely chopped

2 oz (60 g) capers

4 dill pickles (gherkins), finely
    chopped

2 oz (60 g) pitted black olives,
    chopped

4 oz (125 g) stuffed green olives,
    chopped

1 teaspoon chopped chili

1 long French loaf

olive oil

salt and freshly ground black pepper

M • E • N • U
•
Patafla
•
Vitello Tonnato
(page 99)
•
Cheese and Fruit
•

THIS is a lovely Mediterranean picnic loaf — make it the day before to allow the piquancy to develop.

Peel the tomatoes (make two small slits in the skin near the top of the tomatoes and drop into boiling water for about 30 seconds — the skin will peel off easily). Cut the tomatoes into quarters and remove the seeds, then chop and put into a bowl. Combine with the onion, capers, dill pickles, black olives, green olives, and chili.

Cut the French loaf in half lengthwise and scrape out the soft bread inside. Add the soft bread to the other ingredients in the bowl and knead together, moistening with a little olive oil.

Add salt and black pepper to taste, then fill the two halves of the loaf with the mixture.

Press the halves together, then wrap tightly in plastic (cling) wrap and keep in the refrigerator overnight.

Cut into slices to serve.

Serves 6–8

Pickled Garlic and Vinegar Onions

PICKLED GARLIC
2 heads garlic
½ cup (4 fl oz/125 ml) cider vinegar
½ cup (4 fl oz/125 ml) soy sauce
6 teaspoons sugar

VINEGAR ONIONS
onions, preferably purple (Spanish)
onions, finely sliced
sugar
wine vinegar, either white or red

PICKLED GARLIC

THIS is a superb pickle that goes well with all kinds of barbecued or roasted meats. It is an excellent addition to sandwiches and rolls as well.

Peel the cloves of garlic. Put the cloves in one or two jars — you will need about 2 cups (16 fl oz/500 ml) capacity. Bring the remaining ingredients to the boil and simmer until slightly reduced. Pour the hot liquid over the garlic. Allow to cool before sealing. Ideally, keep for three weeks before using, but it can be used sooner.

NOTE: For preserves, the jars need to be thoroughly washed then dried in an oven set to the lowest temperature for about 20 minutes. Once opened, keep pickles in the refrigerator.

VINEGAR ONIONS

THESE onions are terrific with barbecued steak or sausages. Make the quantity you desire — it keeps well in a jar in the refrigerator.

Sprinkle the onions with 1 teaspoon sugar for every onion. Cover with wine vinegar. Leave overnight or longer. Serve using a slotted spoon.

Potato Salad

1 lb (500 g) small new potatoes
2 tablespoons olive oil
1 onion, finely chopped
4 oz (125 g) bacon, diced
2 oz (60 g) bell pepper (capsicum),
    chopped
parsley, chopped

DRESSING
⅓ cup (3 fl oz/90 ml) olive oil
2 tablespoons balsamic vinegar
1 teaspoon French mustard
pinch salt
1 tablespoon mayonnaise

BOIL the potatoes until tender, then drain. Depending on the size, cut into halves, quarters, or leave whole. Put into a bowl and set aside.

Heat the oil and sauté the onion and bacon until the bacon fat is transparent. Add to the potatoes, then stir through the bell pepper and parsley.

Mix the dressing ingredients together thoroughly and add to the salad. Serve at room temperature.

Serves 6

M • E • N • U
•
Duck Liver Paté
(page 37)
•
Cold Roast Beef
•
Potato Salad
•
Mixed Green Salad
•
Apple Cake
(page 13)
•

Salad Niçoise with Fresh Tuna

1 lb (500 g) fresh tuna steaks
½ cup (4 fl oz/125 ml) white wine
8 oz (250 g) French beans
2 medium tomatoes, quartered
1 purple (Spanish) onion, finely sliced
1 Lebanese cucumber, sliced
4 hard-cooked (hard-boiled) eggs, sliced

4 medium potatoes, boiled and
  quartered

DRESSING
4 tablespoons olive oil
2 tablespoons white wine vinegar
2 cloves garlic, finely chopped (minced)
salt and black pepper

M • E • N • U
•
Duck Liver Paté and
Crackers
(page 37)
•
Salad Niçoise
•
Blueberry Sour Cream Cake
(page 27)
•

THIS hearty salad moves into the gourmet class when you use fresh tuna. It's easy to transport the ingredients in separate plastic containers — the salad tastes so much fresher and crisper if you mix it at the last minute. Alternatively, you can arrange the ingredients on serving plates and pour on the salad dressing.

Poach the tuna steaks in the wine for about 5 minutes. You can do this either in a microwave (set on high) or in a covered pan on the stove. Drain and set aside to cool.

Cook the beans in boiling water for about 5 minutes and set aside to cool. Put the beans, tomatoes, onion, and cucumber together in one plastic container. Put the potatoes and eggs in another plastic container. Put the tuna in a container on its own.

Put the dressing ingredients in a jar and shake. When you are ready to eat, toss all the ingredients together and serve with fresh, crusty bread.

Serves 4–6

Salmon and Basil Loaf

1 lb (500 g) canned red salmon
4 oz (125 g) breadcrumbs
2 tablespoons tomato paste (passata)
1 small green bell pepper (capsicum), finely chopped
1 onion, finely chopped
2 tablespoons finely chopped fresh basil

3 eggs, lightly beaten
3 tablespoons vegetable oil
TOMATO COULIS
2 tablespoons olive oil
6 tomatoes, peeled and chopped
1 teaspoon salt
black pepper to taste

THIS dish is good served hot or cold with Tomato Coulis and a green salad.

Put all the ingredients except the oil into a bowl and mix together until well combined. Grease a loaf pan or a fish-shaped mold and pack the mixture into it. Refrigerate for a few hours. Loosen the edges of the loaf with a knife and turn out onto a greased baking sheet. Pour the oil over it.

Bake in a moderate oven (350°F/180°C/Gas Mark 4) for 40 minutes until pale golden brown.

Serves 4–6

TOMATO COULIS

Heat the oil in a saucepan. Add the remaining ingredients. Cover and cook over a low heat, stirring occasionally, for about 15–20 minutes until the tomato is very soft. Stir well before serving.

NOTE: To peel tomatoes, cut two slits in the skin at the stalk end and drop them into boiling water for about 30 seconds. The skin will slip off easily.

M • E • N • U
•
Guacamole and
Corn Chips
(page 87)
•
Salmon and Basil Loaf
with Tomato Coulis
•
Green Salad
•
Cheesecake
•

Scallop Mousse with Avocado

2 avocados, halved and seeds removed
juice of 1 lime
1 small white onion, finely chopped
½ teaspoon Tabasco sauce
parsley, finely chopped
2½ teaspoons gelatin
2 tablespoons water
1 lb (500 g) scallops
¼ cup (2 fl oz/60 ml) white wine

½ teaspoon salt
5 teaspoons gelatin, extra
¼ cup (2 fl oz/60 ml) water, extra
½ cup (4 fl oz/125 ml) thousand
    island dressing (store-bought
    is fine)
1 cup (8 fl oz/250 ml) heavy
    (double) cream, lightly whipped

M • E • N • U
•
Scallop Mousse
with Avocado
•
Chinese Duck Salad
(page 31)
•
Fruit and Cheese
•

SCRAPE the avocado flesh into a bowl. Add the lime juice, onion, Tabasco, and parsley and mash together with a fork. Soften the gelatin in the water and stir over hot water to dissolve. Stir into the avocado mixture. Spread into the base of a non-stick loaf pan and refrigerate.

Poach the scallops in the white wine for about 3 minutes, or until just cooked. Transfer the scallops with the liquid to a food processor or blender. Soften the extra gelatin in the extra water and stir to dissolve over a bowl of hot water. Start the food processor then slowly add the gelatin to the scallops. Scrape the mixture into a bowl then fold through the thousand island dressing and the cream.

Carefully add the scallop mixture to the loaf pan over the avocado layer. Smooth the surface, cover with plastic (cling) wrap and refrigerate until firmly set. To serve, dip into warm water then turn out carefully onto a platter.

Serves 8–10, cut into slices, or many more if passed with crackers

Scallop and Bell Pepper (Capsicum) Salad

1 lb (500 g) scallops
2 tablespoons balsamic vinegar
2 tablespoons vegetable oil
6 scallions (shallots, spring green
    onions), sliced diagonally
1 red bell pepper (capsicum), cut in
    julienne

1 teaspoon chili paste
2 tablespoons walnut oil
rocket (arugola) and chervil for
    serving

PUT the scallops into a microwave container, add 1 tablespoon of the vinegar, cover and microwave on high for 2 minutes (or poach briefly in a pan on the stove). Set aside.

Heat the vegetable oil in a pan and sauté the scallions. Add the bell pepper and the chili paste. Stir briefly then add the liquid from the scallops, turn the heat to high and reduce the liquid in the pan until almost dry. Transfer the scallops to a bowl and add the contents of the pan. Mix the walnut oil with the remaining vinegar and stir through the scallops.

Serve on a bed of rocket and chervil, or any other salad greens that are available.

Serves 4

Shrimp (Prawns) with Mango Mayonnaise

1 lb (500 g) jumbo shrimp (large
    prawns), shelled
1 avocado, cubed
1 small purple (Spanish) onion,
    finely chopped
juice of ½ lime

MANGO MAYONNAISE
2 egg yolks
½ cup (4 fl oz/125 ml) olive oil
juice of ½ lime
1 mango
lettuce, to serve

THIS mayonnaise is delicious with any cold shellfish, or as a dip for
strawberries.

Put the shrimp into a container. Add the avocado cubes and the onion.
Pour the lime juice over the shrimp and mix, stirring gently. Cover with
plastic (cling) wrap and keep cool until ready to serve.

To make the mayonnaise put the egg yolks into a food processor or
blender and start processing. Using a teaspoon, add the olive oil one drop
at a time until about half the oil has been incorporated, then add the rest
in a steady stream. Keep checking the container to make sure that the oil is
being incorporated; if necessary, scrape down the sides. When all the oil
has been incorporated and the mayonnaise is thick and creamy, add the
lime juice.

Peel the mango and cut as much of the flesh away from the seed as you
can — do this over a plate to save the juice. Add the mango flesh and the
juice to the mayonnaise and process until combined.

Serve shrimp on a bed of lettuce with mayonnaise on top or as a dip.

Serves 2 as a main course, 4 as a starter

Smoked Salmon and Guacamole Parcels

GUACAMOLE
1 avocado, halved and seed removed
1 clove garlic, finely chopped
½ small purple (Spanish) onion,
    finely chopped
juice of ½ lemon

½ teaspoon Tabasco sauce
PARCELS
6 slices smoked salmon
Guacamole (see above)
blanched chives

GUACAMOLE without the traditional addition of chopped tomato keeps much better. You can make it a day ahead if you cover it with plastic (cling) wrap pressed on to the surface so there is no air space.

Scrape the flesh of the avocado into a bowl. Add the garlic, onion, lemon juice, and Tabasco and mash together with a fork. Cover with plastic (cling) wrap and refrigerate until ready to use.

Lay the slices of smoked salmon on a board and place a spoonful of guacamole on each one. Fold the salmon over the guacamole to make six parcels. Tie each parcel with blanched chives.

M • E • N • U
•
Smoked Salmon and
Guacamole Parcels
•
Herbed Eye Fillet
(page 49)
•
Pickled Garlic
(page 73)
•
Potato Salad
(page 75)
•
Mixed Green Salad
•
Fruit and Cheese
•

Stuffed Duck in Aspic

10 oz (300 g) ground (minced) pork
    sausage meat (if you wish you
    can use the mince from pork
    sausages)
1 onion, finely chopped
fresh sage, chopped
4 oz (125 g) mushrooms, chopped
4 oz (125 g) pistachio nuts, unsalted

3 cloves garlic, finely chopped
1 boned duck (buy at a specialty
    game store or poultry store)
2 cups (16 fl oz/500 ml) jellied
    chicken stock (buy at a
    poultry store)
½ cup (4 fl oz/125 ml) port wine

THIS elegant dish goes well with Minted Orange Salad (see page 61). It must be kept very cold to prevent the aspic melting, so keep for occasions when the weather isn't too hot.

Combine the pork, onion, sage, mushrooms, nuts, and garlic and stuff the duck with the mixture. Tie the duck with cooking string to make a neat parcel. Prick the skin all over.

Place the duck, breast side up, on a rack in a roasting pan and roast in a moderately hot oven (400°F/200°C/Gas Mark 6) for 30 minutes. Transfer the duck to a terrine dish in which it fits fairly compactly. Add the stock and wine.

Put the terrine dish into a baking dish containing water and return to the oven. Reduce the heat to 350°F (180°C/Gas Mark 4) and cook the duck for another 50 minutes.

Leave to cool then remove the string. Cover and refrigerate.

Remove any fat that sets on top of the jellied stock. Slice the duck and serve cold in its jelly.

Serves 4

Thai Beef Salad

1 lb (500 g) rump steak

DRESSING

2 tablespoons chopped mint leaves

2 tablespoons chopped cilantro (fresh
    coriander)

2 cloves garlic, finely chopped

1 tablespoon soy sauce

1 tablespoon Thai fish sauce

2 tablespoons lime or lemon juice

2 teaspoons sugar

2 small red chilies, finely chopped

1 teaspoon finely chopped ginger

salad greens, to serve

BROIL (grill) the steak for about 5 minutes each side until medium rare. Set
aside to cool.

Mix the dressing ingredients together in a bowl. Slice the steak into
thin strips, add to the dressing and toss to combine.

Serve on a bed of salad greens.

Serves 4

M • E • N • U

•

Cold Avocado Soup
(page 33)

•

Thai Beef Salad

•

Honey Wafers
(page 51)

•

Tomato and Buttermilk Soup

*2 cups (16 fl oz/500 ml) tomato
   juice*

1 cup (8 fl oz/250 ml) buttermilk

THIS simple soup is cool and refreshing; if desired you can add some chopped tomato, cucumber, and fresh herbs. You can also vary the proportion of tomato juice to buttermilk.

Combine the tomato juice and buttermilk.

Serve Tomato and Buttermilk Soup chilled with open sandwiches, which become extra special when you make them with savory butters.

VARIATION: Combine buttermilk and apricot nectar for a refreshing drink.

Serves 2

PINK PEPPERCORN BUTTER: Process butter with pink peppercorns to taste. This is particularly good with roast beef.

ANCHOVY BUTTER: Process butter with anchovy fillets and a little of the oil from the can. This is excellent with chopped hard-cooked (hard-boiled) eggs, watercress, and/or thinly sliced cucumber; it is also good on toast.

HERB BUTTER: Process butter with your choice of herbs; parsley, sage, and cilantro (fresh coriander), are particularly good. Try; sage butter with cold roast chicken or pork, cilantro butter with cold roast lamb, parsley butter with chopped hard-cooked (hard-boiled) eggs.

WALNUT BUTTER: Process butter and walnuts for a butter that is a treat on its own or with other fillings, such as dried fruits, chicken, or cheese.

•

Savory butters are good melted over barbecued meat. Simply shape into a roll, cover with plastic (cling) wrap and refrigerate — cut off slices just before serving and place on the hot cooked meat or fish.

•

Tapenade and Aioli

TAPENADE

5 oz (150 g) good-quality tuna,
    canned in oil
5 oz (150 g) pitted black olives or
    black olive paste
2 cloves garlic
30 g (1 oz) capers

60 g (2 oz) anchovies in their oil

AIOLI

2 egg yolks, at room temperature
6 teaspoons white wine vinegar
1 cup (8 fl oz/250 ml) olive oil
6 cloves garlic

TAPENADE

DRAIN the tuna, reserving the oil. Put the remaining ingredients in a food processor or blender and process. Add the tuna and a little of the oil and process briefly. The ingredients should be mixed but not completely smooth.

AIOLI

Put the egg yolks and 1 teaspoon of the vinegar in a food processor or blender and process until just combined. Continue processing while adding the oil drop by drop, using a teaspoon. Stop and check the processor occasionally to make sure that the oil is being incorporated, scraping down the sides if necessary. When about half the oil has been incorporated you can start adding the rest in a thin stream.

When all the oil has been added and the mixture has thickened, heat the remaining vinegar with the garlic cloves so that the garlic is slightly softened, then add the garlic and hot vinegar to the egg mixture. Process briefly to combine.

NOTE: Heating the garlic cloves with the vinegar prevents the sharp tang that you get when you add raw garlic to mayonnaise. Hot vinegar also makes the mayonnaise lighter and keep better.

•

Some suggestions for accompaniments include: Belgian endive (witloof), steamed asparagus, globe artichokes, parboiled florets of cauliflower or broccoli, carrot sticks, parboiled French beans or lima (broad) beans, celery, fresh grated or parboiled celeriac, raw button mushrooms, fennel, snow peas (mangetout), radishes, zucchini (courgette) sticks, boiled new potatoes, or as a filling for potatoes baked in their jackets.

•

Vegetables Stuffed with Goat Cheese

6 oz (180 g) goat cheese
4 oz (125 g) quark (if unobtainable
  substitute dairy sour cream or
  cream cheese)

8 large cherry tomatoes
3 heads Belgian endive (witloof)
8 button mushrooms

PUT the goat cheese and quark into a bowl and mash together.

Cut the tops off the cherry tomatoes and use a teaspoon to scrape out the seeds and some of the pulp. Fill with some of the cheese mixture.

Separate the endive leaves and fill with some of the cheese mixture.

Remove the stalks from the mushrooms and fill with the remaining cheese mixture.

Arrange on a platter to serve.

Serves 6

M • E • N • U
•
*Vegetables Stuffed with
Goat Cheese*
•
*Shrimp (Prawns) with
Mango Mayonnaise
(page 85)*
•
Cookies
•

Vitello Tonnato with Tuna Mayonnaise

1 nut of veal (this cut from the leg is
    ideal, but you can also
    use fillet)
bacon or pork fat
1 cup (8 fl oz/250 ml) white wine

TUNA MAYONNAISE
2 egg yolks, at room temperature
3 teaspoons lemon juice
1 cup (8 fl oz/250 ml) olive oil
2 oz (60 g) best-quality tuna in oil,
    drained

PUT the veal into a baking dish, cover with bacon or pork fat, and add the
white wine. Roast in a slow oven (325°F/170°C/Gas Mark 3) for about 35
minutes per 1 lb (500 g). Discard the bacon or pork fat and cool.

Carve the veal into thin slices and pack it together in a compact dish. Pour
over the Tuna Mayonnaise (see below), which can be thinned if necessary with
a little juice from the baking dish. Cover and refrigerate overnight.

TUNA MAYONNAISE
Put the egg yolks and 1 teaspoon of the lemon juice in a food processor or
blender and process until just combined.

Continue processing while adding the oil drop by drop, using a teaspoon.
Stop the processor occasionally and check to make sure that the oil is being
incorporated; if necessary, scrape down the sides.

When about half the oil has been incorporated, you can start adding the
rest in a thin stream. When all the oil has been added and the mixture has
thickened, add the tuna and the remaining lemon juice and combine.

Serves 6

Walnut Chicken

6 tablespoons vegetable oil

2 lb (1 kg) chicken pieces

1 onion, finely chopped

2 cloves garlic, finely chopped

1 cup (8 fl oz/250 ml) chicken stock

1 cup (8 fl oz/250 ml) white wine

1 teaspoon salt

6 oz (180 g) walnuts, chopped

basil, preferably purple (opal)

basil, for serving

M • E • N • U

•

Fresh Figs with Prosciutto

•

Walnut Chicken

•

Mixed Green Salad

•

Apple Cake
(page 13)

•

HEAT the vegetable oil in a heavy pan and brown the chicken pieces on one side.

Turn the chicken pieces, add the onion and garlic to the pan, then continue cooking until the chicken pieces are brown on each side and the onion has softened.

Pour off any surplus oil. Add the stock, white wine, and salt, cover the pan, and continue cooking for approximately 30 minutes or until the chicken is cooked through.

Use a slotted spoon to transfer the chicken pieces to a picnic container (preferably shallow, so that the chicken is in one layer) and sprinkle with approximately one-quarter of the walnuts.

Add the remaining walnuts to the sauce in the pan and continue cooking, uncovered, for about 15 minutes until the sauce thickens.

Pour the sauce evenly over the chicken pieces and leave to cool. Cover and refrigerate.

This dish should be made the day before the picnic and served cold, decorated with sprigs of basil.

Serves 6–8

Watermelon and Lychee Salad

¼ watermelon (tiger melon)   ½ bunch fresh mint, chopped
1 lb (500 g) fresh lychees, peeled
2 purple (Spanish) onions, thinely
   sliced

THIS is a cool, refreshing salad that goes beautifully with cold smoked chicken or barbecued fish.

Cut the watermelon into slices or cubes or make balls with a melon baller. Put into a bowl with the lychees (which you can seed if you have time). Keep cold.

Just before serving, gently mix through the mint and onion.

Serves 6

Wild Rice Salad

1 cup (6 oz/180 g) wild rice
2 chicken stock cubes
1 cup (7 oz/210 g) long grain rice
6 tablespoons olive oil

6 scallions (shallots, spring green
   onions), sliced
3 oz (90 g) pine nuts
1 tomato, seeded and chopped

THIS is particularly good with any sort of poultry. Serve warm or at room temperature.

Bring about 4 cups (32 fl oz/1 L) water to a boil in a saucepan, add the wild rice and 1 stock cube and cook, uncovered, over medium heat, stirring occasionally, for 45–50 minutes until tender and the white inside of the seed starts to burst out of the brown skin (or follow the instructions on the pack).

In another saucepan bring about 4 cups (32 fl oz/1 L) water to a boil, add the long grain rice and the remaining stock cube and cook, uncovered, over medium heat for 12 minutes, stirring occasionally.

Meanwhile, heat the olive oil in a pan and sauté the scallions and pine nuts until golden.

Drain the wild rice and long grain rice, then combine both with the scallions and pine nuts.

Mix in chopped tomato.

Serves 8

M • E • N • U
•
Tomato and Buttermilk
Soup
(page 93)
•
Barbecued Atlantic
Salmon with
Pesto Dressing
(page 21)
•
Wild Rice Salad
•
Fruit and Cheese
•

Zucchini (Courgette) and Feta Frittata

3 tablespoons olive oil
4 zucchini (courgettes), thinly sliced
2 onions, thinly sliced
8 eggs

salt and black pepper
4 oz (125 g) feta cheese, cut into
    small dice

FRITTATAS can be made with a wonderful variety of fillings; this version is great served with thin slices of prosciutto, tomato and basil.

Put 2 tablespoons of the olive oil into a non-stick pan (approximately 8 inches/20 cm), then sauté the zucchini and onion for about 15 minutes over a low heat until golden and very soft. Transfer to a bowl and set aside to cool.

Lightly beat the eggs with salt and black pepper to taste.

Wipe the pan with paper towels then add the remaining olive oil and heat. Turn the heat to medium, then pour the eggs through a strainer into the pan.

Spoon the vegetable mixture evenly over the eggs, then add the feta. Leave for about 1 minute, then reduce the heat to low. Cook for 15–20 minutes until the mixture is almost set. Brown the top under a broiler (grill) — about 5–10 minutes.

Serve at room temperature; the piquancy develops well if you make it the day before and refrigerate overnight.

Serves 4 as a main course, or more as a starter

M • E • N • U
•
*Tapenade and Aioli with
Crudités
(page 95)*
•
*Zucchini (Courgette) and
Feta Frittata*
•
*Prosciutto, Tomato and
Basil*
•
*Strawberries
with Balsamic Vinegar
(page 17)*
•

Zucchini (Courgette) Loaf

1 cup (5 oz/150 g) commercial
    baking mix (scone mix)
4 oz (125 g) grated Parmesan cheese
½ cup (4 fl oz/125 ml) vegetable
    oil

4 eggs, lightly beaten
3 zucchini (courgettes), trimmed and
    coarsely grated
1 onion, finely chopped
2 cloves garlic, finely chopped

COMBINE the baking mix and Parmesan cheese in a bowl, then add the
vegetable oil and eggs. Stir until combined. Stir in the zucchini, onion,
and garlic.

Grease a loaf pan and dust lightly with flour. Scrape the mixture into
the loaf pan and bake in a moderate oven (350°F/180°C/Gas Mark 4) for
about 25 minutes, until golden brown. Turn out onto a cake rack to cool.

Serves 6

M • E • N • U
•
*Smoked Salmon and
Guacamole Parcels
(page 87)*
•
Zucchini (Courgette) Loaf
•
*Mushroom Salad
(page 63)*
•
*Blueberry Sour Cream
Cake
(page 27)*
•

I n d e x